Shifting

A Guide To Growing Through The Concrete

LivinPoetry

BookLeaf Publishing
India | USA | UK

Shifting

A Guide To Growing Through The Concrete

© 2021 LivinPoetry

Presentation by *BookLeaf Publishing*

Web: www.bookleafpub.com

E-mail: info@bookleafpub.com

ISBN: 9789358360783

First edition 2021

To my first best friend and eternal angel in the sky who never stopped striving for better, never stopped dreaming, and was never afraid to love with her entire heart.

Acknowledgement

There is multiple people that come to mind when it comes to the creation of this book. To my big sister Ashley who's my best critic and my parachute. No words could properly encapsulate how much your presence in my life means to me so just know you always have my eternal thanks.

To Momma Dukes, the love of my life. Thank you for all you've done for me over the years. Thank you for the lessons, for the advice, for the laughs, and so much more. Thank you for instilling in me the strength to keep fighting, the patience to move mountains, and the determination to rewrite the stars. No matter how far I may go, I will always be your baby bear.

To the House of Le Resistance! Shiann, Hunter, Joia, Toniea, and Kelsey, thank you always for the laughs, the late night heart to hearts, the jokes, the scares and everything in between. I truly adore y'all so much and who knows where I would be without y'all.

To my lovely chosen family that truly spans all nations, all genders, and all abilities. Those who are nearby in an arm's reach and those who are growing and thriving in other parts of the world. Thank you for being the network that keeps me moving through the good days and the bad. For the endless love and support that you pour into me, just know that it never goes unnoticed and I hope that I can pour all of that love into the world just like you all have helped me to thrive.

Preface

To the person that's reading this: May these words help you feel some calm, bring you a moment of joy, and remind you that even if you don't know everything that's on the horizon it'll be okay. You are alive, you are breathing, and you are moving forward towards another day. That in itself is a miracle. Thank you for letting me join you on the adventure and for joining me on my own.

A Guide To Growing Through The Concrete

Past

/ pæst, pɑst /

Noun

1. The series of triumphs and mistakes of those who struggled to breathe that reside as instincts within systems to prevent the termination of beings

2. A tangle of sneaking glances, coded letters of desire, stolen moments of passion, desolate pining, a million page binder of diligently detailed receipts engulfed in the flames of yesteryear

3. A recollection through the dusted tomes through
   overcast concentration and scraps of dissipating
   wonder years that solely remain as tales of yore
   but nothing more

<u>**Preceding Past Perceptions**</u>

Look in the mirror, what do you see?

A pair of darkened lips

painted by my aunt

Rich with traditions of storytelling

children gather round an elder

once evening chores are done

weaving the legends of the ancestors

learn the origins of the arts through the toils of
Africa

dancing, painting, singing, storytelling, to name a
few

ingrained into childhood

A high forehead

entrusted by my mother as

a storage vessel protecting the tome

overflowing tradition's waves

yet waiting to be filled with the hopes of tomorrow

an investment in the future of the motherland

But is this who I am?

Is this really who I am?

For the person I see in the mirror,

is someone I don't know. . .

Where is the person that I saw in my dreams?

The one who was not man nor woman?

The one who lived life to the fullest?

They who confused people

They who lived by their own rules

They who wasn't defined by either

But solely lived as their own person?

That is the person I want to be

This body is not mine

This is not who I am

This frame is merely confinement

Of unfulfilled dreams and more obstacles to
overcome

How do I make that dream a reality?

What must I do?

To break free of the death sentence?

What must I do… To become whole

<u>Opinion</u>

/ ə'pɪn yən /

Noun

1. Whispers sneaking across the lockers as they walk into the halls wearing a cropped top and short skirts that showcases their body hair with a hint of makeup to accentuate their eyes and their short stubble.

2. The unintelligent babble of individuals who haven't done enough soul searching to recognize the pain and trauma they need to grow from to the point that they believe their misconstrued views of a sliver through the looking glass actually means something

<u>A Little One's Knowledge</u>

Why is it that children, no matter what their status are simply loving and open creatures?

Is due to their innate pure nature?

They are born into neutrality that mimics the higher power, that is why they have the knowledge many seek to try and achieve for themselves.

Sometimes when the world is trying to demolish all of our hope and sanity, we need to take a moment to stop and reflect.

Look at the world with the child's eye - it is very beautiful.

We could really learn from children, for they teach us three things:

To find true happiness, we must pull it from within

us

To always be curious and ask questions for clarity

To fight tirelessly for something, even when it

becomes difficult

For as we grow older, we tend to forget that

the child within us never goes away.

The child simply remains there inside,

waiting for that moment to come out and say hello

Insanity

/ ˈdɛr ə lɪkt /

Adverb

1. The spasmodic urge of ashes filling your windpipe as you look at the red stained test score screaming all your worst nightmares back at you

2. The urgent need to slowly dissipate each and every single atom of matter from your body into the very spot your feet rest in the carpet as an elder hurls different expletives towards your direction

3. That irrevocable minute of engulfment into the enormous mammoth of space while simultaneously residing within the last 3600 seconds as your mind glitches into a never-ending loop of sorrow and self sabotage from pursing your lips together in a horrible invocation of defeat by abdication

Insanity Cycles

I hope he's all the wiser

The next guy who ends up with you

Pity, that he won't see through your illusions

Now that I see through your toxic lies.

Another fly in your spiderweb

I was just another toy for you to play with

A piece of property

Tossed to collect dust

When a newer model came around

What's my deal you ask?!

I just don't understand.

No matter how much I try to compromise

We argue in relentless circles

from bills to dinner plans to

who moved the deodorant two stupid millimeters

off center.

Mistakes are made

Tension explodes

Weapons drawn

Wounds reopened

Beaten into submission

Only to recuperate and reach a truce

Apologies are muttered

Excuses made

A state of calm returns

Until Apollo whisks his chariot across the sky

How could I be so oblivious for 2 years?!

Never spotting the glaring omens

The new set of clothes you started to wear

The sudden urge to study more at the library

Now, I know that I was a fool for trusting you

The once sweet smell of lemons is gone.

All that remains is the smell of ammonia.

I look back at the stygian sores peppering my
rachis from the years of stalemates.

All the corrupted moments of bypassing the brick
emblems, ruptures of relationships once cemented
in conviction and baked in credence

…to simply dispose of my being and forsake my
own soul into the dementor's lair.

Loving Guidance

If only you knew

How much it burns me

To see you discouraged

Yet my words mean nothing to you

If only you knew

How much it tortures me

To see you broken

Yet I can't put you back together

I'm here for you, a sentinel on watch

And those lovely eyes made in my heart a notch

Put on duty to protect the priceless art

Yet didn't know these feelings that arose

from the start

Your eyes deserve to twinkle with a glimmer

of starlight

Your laugh deserves to serenade the masses

to a content smile

Your soul deserves to reflect a new rainbow of

compassion after an emotional storm

If only you could see yourself through my eyes
If only you knew how much you truly mean to me

<u>Defying</u>

/ dɪˈfaɪ ənt /

Adjective

1. Elphaba's E6 as it reverberates in the awestruck theatre as she purposely cements her step to freedom

2. The bounce in your step as you strut down the damn street living the absolute best life in the skin your in and not hearing a damn thing that the world gotta say cause you're thriving on going onward with yo lavender!

A Choice for the Future

Well, after 11 years of being in hiding enough is enough. I've tried to hide and put myself in a box for other people and it's time to start living for myself. I wanna thank many of my idols and so many others for helping me to finally be proud and open about myself. To my internet family who has supported me, I love you all dearly. To my childhood friends and family, I love you all dearly. If this is where our relationship ends, then thank you for being a part of my life for as long as you have. So without further ado, I want to introduce myself.

My name is [redacted]. I am 19 years old, and I am a queer person of color. I'm gender fluid, pan-romantic, and demisexual. My preferred pronouns are he/she interchangeably. I love to meet new friends and to give warm hugs. This is who I am and I'm proud. Look out world, this is me."

- September 5th, 2015.

The day that I set the definition of my own element.

<u>Aperture</u>

/ ˈæp ər tʃər /

Adverb

1. Breaking the shackles of regret and distrust that assured you to remain in a dead end job for over 5 years with no sense of growth nor fulfillment as you drive home on a serpentine commute over an hour to open a random mail offer for an interview for your dream job when you finally enter the door of your oasis after a stressful day.

2. Walking out of a situation that used to spiral in your mind in a multitude of universes with hypotheticals and theories, standing on the only solid ground within the expansive quicksand.

3. Cleaning the tears and helping a younger version of yourself navigate through the blind alley. Bandaging their wounds and their basket of lemons on the table. Squeezing the juice out of those lemons, adding some water and a pinch of sugar before mixing together. Pouring the newly made lemonade into some water bottles and sealing the caps. Packing them with some sandwiches into a backpack and putting them on your younger self's back. Kissing their forehead and reminding them that there's a light at the end of this depressive tunnel.

<u>**Some Love For The Past**</u>

Dear younger self,

I want you to know that I'm very proud of you. Back then, we were afraid, worried, confused, a bit frustrated and yet hopeful that when we said these words, something would change. There was a huge risk putting these words onto the internet for all to see...

As I write this right now, we have made it and surpassed the 5th anniversary of this day. We now go by they/them pronouns and don't have a true label. We've gotten more tattoos and piercings, we're freelancing in our field, and we have a chosen family that spans the globe. I remember the fallout and all the chaos that came along with the announcement. There was heartache, there were some lost bridges, and there was a lot of chaos. Our whole world fell apart at the seams, but it unlocked our true self...

It gave us the moment we needed to shed the facade, breath, and start again from scratch.

This journey has been one of the hardest, yet most fulfilling because on that day so long ago, we refused to give their perceptions more power than our reality . I am proud of you for remaining loving through the pain, for being understanding through the misinformation, and for being open despite the many slammed doors in your face.

Don't worry, your people are coming… just continue to search for them for they are also scouring and descrying the expanding and curling path towards you. I swear to you that you are unbelievably stronger than you think and you're just beginning to see what the Divine has in store for you.

Keep going beloved, you got this!

Vulnerable Payoff

It was the hardest choice

To crack open the hard shell facade

And slowly expose the softly thrumming

Drum that had rips and bruises in the skin

To slowly shake out the last remnants of

An ideal opportunity born at an inopportune time

But

With a simple response the heaviest weight

That wedged itself within a forgotten corner

of the skeleton popped out of its place,

eradicating the constant migraine of missed

opportunity and allowing the space to simply jump

off the cliff, spread my wings

and

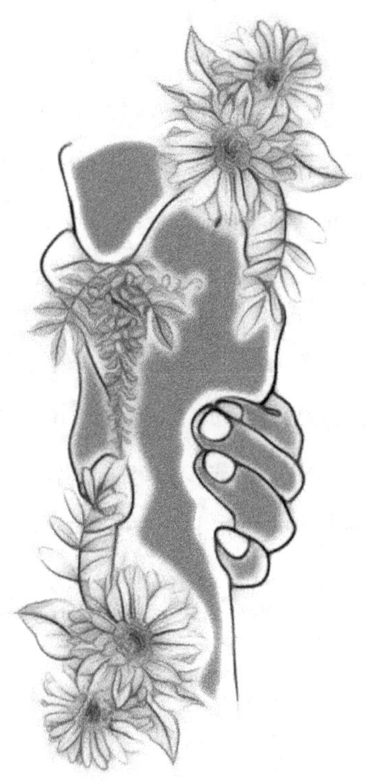

<u>Euphoria</u>

/ yu ˈfɔr i ə, - ˈfoʊr- /

Adjective

1. The elated screams and cheers from around the world as people of colour from sea to shining sea witnessed the birth of Emmy award winner and forever icon Zendaya getting her things for Outstanding Lead Actress in a Drama Series as she rightfully DESERVES!!

2. Slowly awaking from a good night's sleep of your own accord, enjoying the luxurious feel of the sheets brushing against your skin. A soft smile rests on your face as you snuggle a bit deeper under the covers and relax you watch the morning unfold outside your window. The effusive rays of sunlight radiate outward from within your chest as you realised that you are safe, loved, and have everything you need.

Truth

/ truθ /

Noun

1. Sometimes the hardest pill to swallow in the pack

2. An oasis that pushes many thirsty adventurers forward through the desert of life.

3. The only possible thing that will outlast society, the very planet that currently holds life and the ancient ball of fire in the sky

4. Sluggish, yet ever accounted for with the most saccharine of tastes in that final juncture it is dispatched to a congregation of silence awaiting with anxious baited eupnea and all of the bitter notes of backbiting underhanded secrecy is shattered into oblivion.

<u>Truth Shines Even in the Farthest Places</u>

Stars

Sitting under the stars watching them twinkle

Glimmer and gleam

A million stars slowly move overhead

As I remember that I'm not the center of the
Universe

A small dot in the vast expanse of the never-ending
space

Underneath the darkness of night

With nothing except the stars above me

It's quite amazing to realize

These stars have outlived us

They have been here since the beginning of time

The same stars that we all share

No matter where we may be in the world

Many have witnessed things that we would never understand

How many of them made the dreams of children into reality?

How many of them blessed the union of new couples?

How many of them silently lead many slaves towards freedom?

How many of them heard the prayers of the Palestinians?

How many of them watched as humans fought their compatriots for some semblance of sovereignty?

Many connect together to represent figures of the past

Each one having a backstory that sometimes vary in language

Yet the story remains uncensored and unedited

Mother Nature's own masterpiece that can never be replicated

As steadfast as the constellations that never change their ways

May we too stay on the path of truth

Never faulted by distortion of fact

Never dominated by dishonesty

Never swayed into tranquility by misrepresentation.

<u>An Heir's Fight For Their Kingdom</u>

Who am I?

It's absolutely terrifying when you have not an

inkling of sense in regards to your identity

I mean, I'm not trying to be needy but I really feel

like I need to ask

Who am I?

Cuz it seems like I no longer know for myself. . .

In this world where somehow and someway

someone else has the power to determine

If I am legitimate or not

Someone else has the power to determine

If I am worthy or not

Someone else has the power to decide

If my life matters or not

Someone else has the power to choose

If my history is important or not

Someone else has the power to designate

If my voice is substantial or not

All because of this one little power called privilege

And no matter how much I try to push through

No matter how much I try to move forward

No matter how much I try to keep swimming

It feels like I've hit a wall.

I'm forced to take on another language to offset my
natural dialect

Yet I'm judged no matter how I portray myself

If I speak with proper enunciation and an arsenal of
vocabulary

I am deemed as someone trying to remove
themselves from their past

If I speak with the slang of my natural dialect and
the rhythm of my culture

I am deemed unintelligent and another "loud and rude black person"

If I decide to protect my hair with a simple weave

I'm deemed as trying to fit the white beauty standard

But if I decide to let my natural hair breath

I'm deemed unprofessional and unkempt

My brothers can no longer walk the streets

Without fearing for their lives

My sisters can no longer go out for the night

Without fearing for their bodies

My identity is invalidated

My experiences are ignored

My voice is oppressed

And yet I should keep quiet?

I should plaster a smile on my face like everything
is ok?

I should simply be happy that I'm able to attend
this institution

Where they fill me with their education

They ignore the knowledge that I've gained

They deem what I know as barely subpar

They tell me that this is what I need to know

Yet they cover up the injustice

They hide the flaws of the first world

They emphasize the importance of knowing "your
history"

But tell me, where is my history?

Where are my Black leaders that struggled for their
basic rights?

Where are my Indigenous speakers who used their
knowledge to educate the masses about racial
equality?

Where are my Caribbean singers who reminded us about the trials and tribulations of the past?

Where are my Latinx writers who wrote about living in a better world?

Where does my diaspora exist when the colonisers continue to scrub us out of existence?

We keep losing more and more lives each day

And yet we're supposed to remain quiet

We're supposed to keep a smile plastered on our face

We're supposed to become complacent. . .

No.

I will continue to fight

I will continue to scream

I will continue to protest

To educate those who are willing to listen

To call out those who abuse their privilege

To articulate the problematic ties of the patriarchy
and their rod of systematic oppression

To encourage my fellow activists

And to fight for those who also deal with
oppression

I refuse to be ignored anymore.

I.

Will.

Not.

Be.

Silenced.

I live for the day

I live for the day

Where I don't have to worry

About my nieces and nephews

Running around free as air

Might lose their magical light

As they bleed to their deaths

From a bullet to their chest

I live for the day

Where I don't have to grieve

As I check in with friends

Calling and tensely hoping

Just to hear their voice

Rather than their name

In a news headline

I live for the day

Where I can walk outside

And enjoy the long peaceful day

Without watching my back

Fearful of people

Without dissolving into the crowd

Just to make it home safely

I live for the day

Where my hair isn't made into a zoo exhibit

As I shift with the energy that's passed down

Into prayers and meditations of safe passage

From ancestors and guides that protect me

Pulled down from the stars and weaved into my
mane

By skillful mediums whose magic rest within their
hands

I live for the day

And I'm not asphyxiating under the gaze of

A beast dressed in the terrorists uniform of blue

Hungrily ransacking roads and streets for more
prey to sink their teeth in

Insolent harbingers of a system that drills deep into
the

Rich brown earth and claims the culture, the food,
the clothing, the speech

Yet refuses to stand in their ""blackness"" when the
shit hits the fan

I live for the day

When I don't have to cry anymore

Shedding tears in a solemn prayer

For the lost souls gone too soon

For the families with gouged out hearts

Trying to mend their souls back piece by piece

From a loss that was made in cold blood

I live for the day

I live for the day

I live for the day

Where I wouldn't have to make

Hopeless supplications to a Divine Just to live with my people without a target on our backs

I live for that day...

<u>Nix</u>

/ nɪks /

Interjection

1. The expeditious way to unveil all the creatures that venture by the moonlight for slandering the numinous aliases of the Divine Night

2. A moment of withdrawal to access the present situation and gather affirmation of the summation of moments which resulted in this cessation

3. The dynamism to face the most heinous, oppressive fractures of the world without succumbing under the narcotic albatross

4. An elucidation of its own merit without further arousal

A ~~Queen's? King's?~~ Monarch's Ascent

As the midnight hour rises

I feel something within myself stir

The seal to the forbidden side obliterated

My real spirit begins to awaken

The mind runs on overdrive

As my eyes reflect the light of the moon

A shifting within the body

As powers from another realm slip

Through to enter the living and

Sever the connection between

The machine of lies that powers the corrupt
overmaster of greed and

Unleash the secluded energy of the ethereal
patchwork surrounding me.

<u>Final Invitation</u>

If i opened up

Opened the safe inside

Put down the drawbridge

Lead you over the moat

Let you in past the gate

Allow you to wander the halls

Gaze at the walls of my past

Will you pillage my castle?

Will you follow the halls?

Walk into the foyer

Strut past the statues

Up the grand staircase

Down the sacred halls

To the end of the hall

To the Quing's crystal bedroom door

And saunter your way inside?

Or will you walk past the grand hall

Stroll down to a lower level

Roam around and through the kitchen

File down the stairs two by two

Through the maroon dungeon door

Trek the twist and turns of the labyrinth of my
heart

To the centre of the room

Where you'll learn that the true ruler

Is the werewolf that hides within

Chasing Legacies

*"How do you want to be remembered? As a sinner
or a saint?"*

*"I want to leave my footprints on the sands of
time"*

"Legacy, Legacy what is a legacy??"

There is this focus on how we will be remembered

When our time on this plane has reached its end

Maybe it's an innate part of our experience

To look towards the end of something or

Maybe it's a method to deal with the perplexing
thought

That we are merely drops in the waterfalls of time

As I try to plant my roots into the current of today

A small piece of me grows into an entity of its own

Stretching out its incandescent scaly arms

Breathing sparks of curiosity through the void

Soaring off through the horizons of the mind as

It chases the shiny flicker of a drift to add to it's
collection

The words echoing each night when I shut my eyes
to rest

Will my words fall on deaf ears or

*Will they somehow spill out of the chasms of notes
that*

*I pour my heart into and gain the autonomy to go
out*

*and search for the people who can make sense of
them*

rather than wilting in the hands of

those who claim they can read it

Fighting Historical Legacies

If people losing their families doesn't make you mad

If children going hungry doesn't ignite something in your soul

If families becoming homeless doesn't create a rage in your stomach

If the blatant bigotry in this nation doesn't make you absolutely furious

Then I have one question for you to consider:

When the generations of the future look back on this time of change

Will you be on the right side of history?

<u>Curiosity</u>

/ ˌkyʊər iˈɒs ɪ ti /

Interjection

1. The proclaimed winner of the battle against the cat, yet the cat still had eight more lives to fight on once again

2. A older person's more polite way of challenging the audacity of the youth today to be more unbiased in how they and other individuals decide to live their lives so long as it isn't causing any harm to anyone else

3. That sensation in the base of the brain that branches off to connect with the spine as something inside slowly begins to tingle like a seed sprouting through the hard shell and growing from the harvesting of insight to eventually thrive as the once obscure mirror slowly becomes much more clear

<u>A Break of Curiosity</u>

What? How? What? Where? How? Where? Why? Where? Where? How? How? Why? Who? How Much?? Who? Which? Who? What? Why? How? How Often??? Where?

Phrases that set a spark through the continuum of psyche to formulate

On a concept through the alchemy of weaving letters into an elaboration of

Phrases which can bind together to build up mountains and destroy villages but

does anyone ever

Take the split moment of a leaf sailing on the sliver of air to wonder

When do we decide to exchange our eagerness to broaden our horizons

Through the acquisition of ideas that we only
dreamed of to a sphinx like

Merchant with muted wings for purloined seconds
to cement our feet and continue

To slowly lug our packs overflowing with torment,
trial, and dilemma on this finite earth

How? Why? What? What? What? Which? Who? Why?
Who? Often??? Much? How Much??? Why? Much?
Why? Where? How Where? How? Where? How?
Which?? Who? What? Where?? Why? How?

<u>Compliments to the best parts of you</u>

The parts of you that reflect out into the world yet

You can't see fully cause you solely reside in you

The part of you that still wakes up each morning

despite the toxicity around you

The part of you that puts one foot in front of

the other each day

The part of you that keeps trying to do better when

the world seems to be doing worse

Give yourself a moment to breathe

Relax your shoulders

Let go of that tension

You're doing amazing because you're doing something that no one has EVER done before

You're simply being you and that is more than enough

The sun is shining a bit brighter

The grass is a bit greener

The birds are singing a bit sweeter

All because you're here with us and gracing us with your beautiful self.

I'm so happy that you're still here

<u>**Flowers For The Living**</u>

Flowers seemed to be reserved for those greats

After they have breathed their final breath in this
plane

Botanical capsules of the macrocosm given to
eulogize

those who have left a black hole within a chamber
the size

Of their presence.

Why do we wait til the end of

Our time to remind and reminisce about

All the things one has done in minutes past?

Why do we hold in our affirmations and Feelings of
encouragement with tense breath

As if our words would give way to Medusa's fatal
curse??

Take time to let the ones who means the most

To you how you perceive them.

Don't await the ultimate conclusion to pour your

feelings into

Your dear ones for you will solely take with you

Empty moments of hypothetical and sorrow when

You can embrace them now and feel that Care

stitched together surround you in soothing love

And those seeds that you plant

Into others shall grow with tending

Until they sprout and blossom in due time

In turn they will plant their seeds which

Could become the roses in the concrete

That will lead to the oak trees rooted in the rivers

Showering this world in more love and unity.

<u>Bad Weather</u>

/ bæd ˈwɛð ər /

Interjection

1. A bop by the queen Kirstin™ from the LOVE EP (it's a great song, give it a listen!)

2. Old classification of storms that were given feminine names for weathermen to equate emotions and vulnerability with destructive behaviour

3. Code name for one of the baddest and most incredible superheroes to ever grace the world with her determination, her regal manner and her tactical nature

4. Those who have learned to dance across the
   tightrope of masculine and feminine qualities
   with a comfort that fills them with the power to
   make the ground quake with the steps, whip
   heads around with their presence, and control
   the tides of hearts with their words. Those who
   glow with a white light of rarity for their
   potential to shift this world anew.

<u>**Cloudbursts Centrum**</u>

"You are tuned in and turned on

To who you really are

You have a unique and important purpose

A mission your soul has come here to discover" -
Qveen Herby

"Oh, I can't fit their mold

No, we can't take on that wall

'Cause they'll talk about us

Like we're bad weather" - Kirstin

"You deserve the world and if no one else will say
it

Then I'll spit it to the mic in the studio when I lay it

Now play it when you discouraged

I know chasin' the impossible take some courage

And I can promise at the end of your journey

When it's all said and done

Won't nothin' feel much better then hearin',

""My nigga, you won""

Aye!" - CHIKA

Women who have taken the cold, dry air of the world's negativity, used it as fuel for their hustle to grow more powerful, embraced every part of them, emotions and all to boost them to newfound heights and become the Storm.

Today is the day. Today is challenge day!

An annual thing in the calendar from the day that I first breathed in this world.

Today is the day that I say goodbye to the old me.

Goodbye to the past doubts and issues.

Goodbye to regrets and failed relationships.
Goodbye to blame and all those lost chances

We line up at the start.

I lace up my shoes extra tight so I won't trip over worry.

I stretch my legs, going up the body so I don't tense in anxiety.

I take a deep breath admitting myself to breathe in possibility and expel the negativity.

My opponent snarls from their spot and I line up at the start

When that horn blares, I run.

Run towards happiness

Run towards love

Run towards healing

My opponent falls behind and resides in the past as
I sprint towards my goal of a higher version of
myself laying beyond the limitless horizon.

<u>Good Morning!</u>

Can I just say that it's a miracle to see you again?

So much could've happened and yet here you are again!

You are your ancestor's wildest dreams.

Everything they worked and strived for led to you!

Today is a new page in this chapter of your life.

Another moment to make match your heart's content

Can I tell you a secret??

You, yes YOU, are the only person who holds the pen

So, what are you gonna write today??

Thank you once again for picking up this piece of me and bringing it into your world. I hope that it can serve as some sort of solace for you in whatever form you may need and it remind you that you aren't alone in this divisive time.

We're all going through changes and trying to piece ourselves back together in one of the most confusing and complex times. Please take a moment to recognize that your feelings are valid, no matter if you wanna bury into your home and never leave or if you're ready to safely try and connect back in the world.

There's no one path to the next steps here. Shoo,
I'm also trying to figure it out as I go. One thing
that isn't disputed though is that you are loved.
You are loved and supported more than you know,
just reach out and tap into the love when needed. It
may not come immediately, but I promise if you
keep your eyes and ears open, the love will come
back to you when you least expect it.

*9 7 8 9 3 5 8 3 6 0 7 8 3 *